African Mythology

Gods and Mythical Legends of
Ancient Africa

Table of Contents

Introduction

A ncient Africa holds a rich legacy of oral cultures, philosophies, and standards that reflect today's deep moral standards. For centuries, African mythology has largely been overlooked by its Western neighbors, particularly Greece and Rome, where myths and legends are typically narrated as single stories, unlike their African counterparts. But in recent years, academics and popular readers are starting to steer back to this continent, where legends and deities from ancient civilizations are just waiting to be revealed to the world.

What makes African myths different from Western or even Asian mythology is that legends here tend to be infused and retold through ritual practice, even centuries after first told. We can see this throughout the continent, from north to south and east to west.

The universe tends to be depicted anthropomorphically, with human bodies acting as a miniature version of the essential elements and forces that the universe is made up of. We can see this clearly in twinship, a theme that runs throughout the African continent, particularly in Western African legends, since human bodies are seen as the 'twin' of the universe.

In Mali, several ethnic groups such as the Dogon, the Malinke, and the Bambara, believe that the first people to exist were actually twins, and twins are still considered the 'ideal.' When a baby is born, the placenta is seen as the child's twin, and the place where their soul and destiny are located, is buried within the family ground's and then sprinkled with water.

The Asante ethnic group considers twins of such high regard that they are almost regarded as living shrines, nearly sacred beings, and a living symbol of fertility. However, traveling further down the continent to the Democratic Republic of the Congo, we see that twins are a symbol of excessive fertility within the animal kingdom instead of the human or divine worlds, and ceremonies and rites are conducted to safeguard their people from this strange ailment.

Another common theme seen in African mythology from ancient times to the present is that of a trickster figure. These beings are infamous for their mischievous and sometimes deadly pursuits, full of lust, enormous appetites, and bringing chaos to order. But even with this, they tend to introduce a new, vibrant and energetic order to the world around them. Legba, a trickster being worshiped for centuries by the Fon of Benin, may bring trouble to the land and their people but is worshiped as a being that brings transformation to them and isn't regarded as a wicked being. He is revered as the messenger of the Supreme Being, Mawu. As a result, tricksters are a representation of the constantly ordained universe, grounded and stable, yet constantly changing all the time.

Africa is a continent made up of 54 countries, with thousands of years of history and cultures, and more than a thousand languages are spoken here today. Since the dawn of history, this amazing place has seen the rise and fall of countless cultures and civilizations, each with its own set of beliefs and pantheons of deities. No one corpus of myths and legends unite this vast place, but many regions will share a set of common elements.

The history of Africa is rich and varied. Several kingdoms and cultures are better known than others, such as Egypt and Ethiopia because they were recorded by other cultures like Greece and Rome, who have left us with written sources. Other kingdoms are known because their monuments and structures have survived.

Some of the most famous ancient kingdoms include Egypt, Ta-Seti (northern Nubia), Kush, Cathage, the Berbers, Macrobia, Aksum, the Ghana Empire, and the Nok culture, which allowed the development of the Sao, the Kanem Empire, and Bornu Empire in the medieval period.

Just as in other parts of the world, African myths and legends reflect the values and beliefs of the people from ancient times, but unlike other areas of the world, these myths still play a vital part in African people's daily lives today.

Chapter 1:

The Roots and Origins of African Mythology

U nlike the myths and legends of the Classical World (ancient Greece, Rome, Britain, etc.) and that of Asia, much of our knowledge of ancient African cultures and civilizations have come through oral traditions that are still practiced or were recorded in the 18th and 19th centuries through European missionaries. Like the myths from ancient Egypt, some are recorded on ancient monuments that have survived the ravages of time.

The Sahara Desert, a large expanse of glistening golden sands, stretches across the northern part of the African continent from east to west. In ancient times, this region, from Morocco to Egypt and then running down to Ethiopia, was referred to as North Africa. The cultures here traded with other civilizations all across the Mediterranean and the ancient Middle East, all of whom had a deep influence on the religious beliefs of the natives. Christianity came to North Africa during the fourth century CE, and then Islam during the eighth century CE.

The rest of the African cultures below the Sahara Desert did not have much contact with the world until modern times. Islam may have swept across North Africa relatively quickly, but they failed to have the same influence beyond here for a long time. Their Christian counterparts experienced the same and didn't have a great influence south of the Sahara until the late 19th century.

However, once both Islam and Christianity did manage to gain ground, their influences tended to overshadow and dominate many of the native religions, forcing the centuries of myths and legends to disappear entirely in some places.

In other locations, though, the traditional gods, goddesses, spirits, and legendary figures have survived, either on their own or through the blending with other religions from outside cultures. As a result, it is possible to see some African Muslims combine ancestral worship with Islam or African Christians blending Christian beliefs with traditional beliefs.

Sub-Saharan mythology is the product of thousands of years of worship and transformation. Such changes can be seen through mass migrations that occurred over the centuries. Around 7,000 years ago, the Khoisan ethnic group's ancestors migrated from around the Sahara and headed south. Around 2,000 years, Bantu-speaking Africans started to migrate from modern-day Cameroon on the west coast of Africa until they dominated the Sub-Saharan region. These migrations led to a transference of mythology from one region to another, influencing other ethnic groups along the way, until there was a melting pot of legends and spiritual beliefs.

But as with myths and legends from other places, these mass migrations led to a rise in legends regarding historical figures and events. This gives us an insight into times, places, and events that are not recorded within books, scrolls, or monuments and increases our knowledge and understanding of history.

Most African cultures didn't use written languages until recently. History and stories were passed down orally, from one generation to the next. For thousands of years, there were groups of people who would be in charge of keeping a record of their people's history through storytelling – and even continue this today.

The first written accounts of African myths and legends first appeared in the early 19th century when colonizers and missionaries from Europe started to make their way through the continent. For the last century, there has been a surge of interest in scholars to document these gods, myths, and legends before they disappear to changes within African cultures and identities.

Important Gods and Characters

Ancient African mythology includes a vast array of gods and supernatural figures, and creatures that greatly influence the day-to-day lives of humans.

Not only do the gods do this, but ancestral spirits and lesser gods.

The majority of ancient African cultures have a pantheon of gods, commonly placed together and identified as families. Most of these cultures and civilizations will recognize one deity as all-powerful, the Supreme Being, and is usually associated with the heavens of the sky. In West Africa, many ethnic groups even today recognize this deity as Olorun or Amma, and over in East Africa, they tend to refer to this deity as Mulungu. For ethnic groups who have now embraced Christianity or Islam as their dominant religion, they will sometimes blend the ancient deity with the newer faith.

Even from ancient times, African deities who are seen as the supreme God are rarely involved with the daily lives of humans and are rarely called upon. Instead, ancient and modern-day Africans would call upon the lesser-powerful gods, deities who have distinctive roles to play.

Chapter 2:

Spirits

S pirits have played an integral role in ancient Africa's mythology and continue to do so even in the present days. Spirits are invisible beings who hold great powers that can be used for positive or negative actions. They have less power than deities but aren't quite as emotional or weak as humans. They also tend to be identified with features in the landscape, such as mountains, springs, rivers, and trees, and were often worshipped well beyond the limits of their culture's borders.

Unlike elsewhere, ancient Africans believed that plants and animals, just like humans and the elements, had a spirit. Some spirits were benevolent, and others were more destructive. Throughout history, some of these spirits were thought to be witches. Some tribes and cultures would try to influence and control the damage they wrought through magic, typically with a shaman's help, a highly respected individual known for their healing and magical abilities.

Since the earliest times, African myths reinforce the belief in life after death. Throughout the various African cultures, some stories share the common belief that their spirit dwells within an upside down underground world when a human dies. During the day, these spirits will sleep and then emerge after the sun goes down. In other cultures, the spirit world was located in the sky. For centuries, the Bushmen of South Africa believe that their spirits become a star when one of them dies.

Throughout African history, it was also believed elsewhere that the spirits of the dead would linger near their living family, acting as protectors and guides. For thousands of years, Africans would perform rites and ceremonies to honor their ancestors, particularly with powerful chieftains. Reincarnation has been a long-held belief, with myths and legends recounting how one individual's spirit was reborn as a baby or as a snake – both themes are common in ancient myths.

Ancestral worship has been performed for thousands of years and has been an integral part of Eastern and Southern African mythologies. Because they are still practiced today, it allows us more understanding of the ancient beliefs, the stories, and ceremonies that their ancestors performed centuries earlier. Once a human being who made his son a chieftain, Zoa is still worshiped as the divine protector of the Songhai people.

Since antiquity, African cultures traced their origins to either a pair of humans or a single individual, their ancestors. In modern-day Uganda, the Baganda state that Kin tu was the first being who emerged from the land where the gods resided to marry Nambi, the heavenly king's daughter. According to the Dinka in Sudan, the Supreme Being created a pair of small clay figures who became the first humans – Garang and Abuk.

But even spirits had the ability to transform into more powerful beings. Ancient kings and even legendary heroes of ancient times could sometimes turn into deities, albeit lesser ones, who were worshipped by entire cultures and kingdoms. They start as human beings whose deeds and actions were either revered or reviled to such an extent that they stepped over the line separating humans and gods to become divine themselves. The ancient Yoruba god Shango, a storm god, is believed to have originated as a powerful warrior king whose legend become so legendary that his descendants lifted him up to godship – a common motif not only in African mythology but in mythologies all over the world.

Chapter 3:

Twin Myths

E ven from the earliest times, twins have been considered almost sacred. They were a representation of the duality of nature – the balance between the human world and the 'other world,' the representation of the cosmos, the harmony between opposite forces. Male and female pairs of twins have been the ideal symbolism of this.

Male and female twins reoccur within African mythology, many of which are seen as brothers and sisters who come together, marry, and populate the world. Other stories state that they are two sides to one human being. Mawu-Lisa, the Supreme Being of the Fon people in West Africa, is believed to have originated as a pair of male-female twins and gave birth to the rest of the gods.

While most of the continent saw the birth of twins as a blessing, there were other cultures and kingdoms that considered them a bad omen or worse. Since antiquity in modern-day Nigeria, the Igbo speaking groups have been scared of twins. They were considered supernatural beings sent by the gods who could devastate their way of life. According to mythology, the Earth goddess stated to the people that they were an offense and had to be destroyed. If the people didn't, then her anger would be let loose on all the people. As a result, many twins were placed within earthenware pots and left within the forest.

Not far away in the same country, the Yoruba welcomed the arrival of twins. According to mythology, the God of thunder and lightning, Shango, is the protector of twins. Throughout history, the Yoruba treated twins with such honor and reverence that they were almost seen as sacred beings. If they were not treated well, however, and one or both died, it would bring misfortune to not just their family but the entire community. When one or both twins did die, an Ibeji statue would be carved, and the parents would look after, sing, and love the statue as they would their living child; those who didn't would go on to suffer great misfortunes. Ibeji statues have been found throughout Nigeria dating well back into the Iron Age, testifying the great significance twins played within ancient African religious beliefs and continuing to do so even today.

Perhaps two of the most recognized twins are that of the goddess Nut and Geb, who formed the sky and earth in ancient Egyptian mythology. As well as being brother and sister, they were also husband and wife who wouldn't take part to allow life to flourish. The sun god Ra was finally able to separate them using air, with Nut stretched across the heavens and Geb stretching beneath her. Depictions show them still united at either end of their bodies, forming a whole.

While twins are commonly depicted as lovers or husbands and wives, several myths depict them as rivals. Osiris and Set, Nut and Geb's twin sons, competed with each other even before they were born. Set was determined to be the firstborn that he fought his way out of his mother's womb, even though he wasn't fully formed. The rivalry didn't end there, though, and he hated his brother to such an extent that he finally killed him and scattered the pieces of his dismembered body throughout the land. Again, as with elsewhere, this myth clearly shows the duality of nature and the universe, not physically as with Osiris' and Set's parents, but as moral forces.

This theme of twins as the origins of the universe continues further south in Mali. To the Dogon, twins have been regarded as the ideal for thousands of years. Nunmo, a deity long worshipped by the Dogon and considered whole or complete, was actually a set of male and female twins who sacrificed one part of themselves to create the world and the rest of the deities. And, as such, the rest of the gods lacked Nunmo's sacred wholeness.

For the Fon people, the God Mawu-Lisa started out as a set of male and female twins; Mawu represents the moon and is female, and Lisa as the male sun element. Together, they birthed the rest of the gods, who were also sets of twins.

Chapter 4:

Creation Myths

C reation myths are an important element of any culture's religious and social identity. They represent how these ancient peoples believed the world to exist, and since some include grains of actual history, they are vital to our knowledge of world history.

But while many cultures and kingdoms throughout Africa had their own unique beings with different names and creatures, there is a common element that can be identified with other civilizations around the world, illustrating that humans, no matter where you go, share more than what they think.

African Bushmen Creation Myth

The Bushmen of the southern region of Africa – primarily South Africa, Botswana, Angola, and

Namibia – have lived in this area for thousands of years.

People didn't live on the Earth's surface. Every human and animal dwelled beneath the ground, overseen by the Great Master and Lord of All Life, Kaang. Life was peaceful, and people lived in harmony without greed and not wanting for anything. And even though they lived underground, their kingdom was always bathed in light. Looking over his paradise, Kaang decided to make the land above a second paradise for his people.

Kaang started by creating a magnificent tree that had branches that stretched over the whole land. He then started to dig a hole near the base of the tree, which eventually reached the underground land where his subjects and all the animals dwelled.

Once he had finished creating the world as he saw fit, he started to lead the first man through the hole. Sitting beside it, it didn't take long before the first woman appeared. When everyone had emerged and stood beneath the tree, they looked in surprise and wonder at the world around them. Kaang then began bringing the animals up through the hole; some were so excited about the world that they climbed through the trees' roots and emerged through the actual branches.

When all the animals and people were out of the hole, Kaang gathered them around him and told them to live in harmony with each other. He instructed the people not to create fire; otherwise, they would suffer a wicked evil. The humans promised they would not build any fires, and Kaang retreated to a location that allowed him to watch over his people without them seeing him.

When the sun started to dip beneath the horizon and night swept its dark cloak across the sky, every human being started to feel the icy grasp of fear around their hearts. In the darkness, they could not see each other. On the other hand, the animals possessed the eyesight to see in the dark, and their fur coats kept them warm. Cold and scared, the humans wondered what they should do. One man said maybe they should build a fire in order to keep warm. In their eagerness to stay warm, they forgot about Kaang's warning and created a fire. It wasn't long before they could see each other again, and they were warm.

Despite this, though, the animals feared the fire and ran away, fleeing into the mountains and caves to hide. Since this day, humans have lost the ability to talk with the animals who now fear humans.

The Yoruba of Nigeria

Nothing existed in the world but the sky, the earth, and water. The great God Olorun ruled everything in the world. Obatala, another god, sought out Olorun and requested permission to create a place where living things could survive. Olorun granted this wish and consulted Orunmila, his eldest son, about it. Orunmila instructed him to find a chain made out of gold and a snail's shell that contacted corn, palm nuts, sand, and an egg that contained the essences of male and female orishas.

Finding the gold chain, Obatala used the chain to descend from the sky down to earth but couldn't go any further than the length of the chain. He took the snail's shell and poured the sand within it to create dry land. While he was doing this, he dropped the egg, releasing Sankofa (a mythic bird that flies forward while looking back). When there was enough land, Obatala used the rest of the sand to create more earth and then placed the pine nuts within it. Lonely by himself, he formed humans and created Ife, the first city where the gods would visit regularly.

Zimbabwe

Modimo was the creator of the world and symbolized the good within it. However, he had a dual nature and could be a destructive force, bring devastation and natural disasters to the land when angered. When he was pleased, he lived in the east and was represented by water; when angered, he lived in the west and represented by fire. Myths claim he created the earth, roots, light, and the sky.

Zulu

According to the Zulu, the first God to exist was Unkulunkulu (the Ancient One). He was formed by uthlanga, or reeds, and brought forth humans and animals. Afterward, he fashioned the world and the rest of the living things within it. He then instructed the Zulu how to make fire and to hunt and feed themselves. The Zulu believe that everything he created is a part of him.

Egypt

There are a few versions of the ancient Egyptian creation myth.

In the beginning, there was nothing but darkness and chaos. No one but Heka (the God of magic) existed, who was waiting for creation to begin. The universe was an endless stretch of dark, murky water. From out of here emerged a great primeval hill called ben-ben. The God Atum stood upon this hill and, realizing that he was alone, became pregnant with his own shadow using magic. He first spat out Shu, the God of air, and then vomited Tefnut, the goddess of moisture. Shu gave life rules, and Tenfnut gave the order.

Shu and Tefnut left their father on the primeval hill and started to fashion the world. When they had been gone for a long time, Atum started to fear for them and sent out his own eye so it could look for them. While it was searching, Atum sat on the hill and thought about the universe.

When Shu and Tefnut finally returned, they gave him back his eye. Overjoyed and relieved with seeing his children, Atum started to cry. When these tears fell onto the rich earth, they created the first men and women.

However, these human beings didn't have a place to live. Shu and Tefnut became lovers and gave birth to the God Geb and the goddess Nut, who formed the earth and sky. Geb and Nut were deeply in love and wouldn't part from their embrace but Atum did not approve of this and separated them, pushing Geb below and Nut above. The two lovers were able to see each other but couldn't touch. Nut was already pregnant and later birthed Osiris, Set, Isis, Nephthys, and Horus, the five deities who formed the earliest version of the Egyptian pantheon. Osiris was considered to be the most just and wise of the gods, and Atum gave him the world to rule over before he finally retreated from the world.

The Akan of Ghana

The Akan people of Ghana and the Ivory Coast trace their origins to Nana Nyame, who lived up in the heavens while the goddess Abrewa and her offspring dwelled upon the earth. To reach Nana Nyame, they prepared food, but the God wasn't pleased with this, so they moved higher up in the heavens. However, Abrewa requested her children to create a large tower made of mortar. Slowly, they placed one layer of mortar upon the other, stretching high into the sky. Just before they reached Nana Nyame, they ran out of mortar, so Abrewa told them to use the bottom layer. Her children did this, and the tower collapsed, leading to the suffering of her children.

The Berbers of North Africa

The Berbers are an ethnic group who live primarily in the northwest part of Africa and can trace their roots back to before Islam swept through the region.

According to them, a single man and woman dwelled beneath the earth before creation began.

They didn't realize they were different until they started arguing at the drinking well. The woman insisted that she drink from it first, but the man shoved her. Landing on the ground, her clothes rose up, and the bottom half of her body was revealed. When the man asked about her body, she told him that her body symbolized goodness.

For eight nights, they stayed together, producing fifty sons and fifty daughters. Because of the number of children they had, they sent the above. There, they became the first people to inhabit the land, and their numbers swelled.

The Oromo of Ethiopia

The largest ethnic group in Ethiopia, the Oromo, has lived in East Africa since the dawn of history. According to myths, the creator of the Oromo was Waqa, who lived high up in the sky and remained separated from Earth using the stars as a barrier. Although he didn't punish the people when they were bad, he did resort to tricking or persuading them.

He made a request man fashion him a coffin. When it was finished, he placed them within it and placed it on a flat expanse of land. He then called forth a magnificent rainstorm that continued for seven years, which then molded and shaped the earth.

When the rainstorm subsided, the man was allowed to depart the coffin. Using his blood, he fashioned a woman. Thirty children were born to these women, but the man decided there were too many, and Waqa transformed fifteen of them into animals.

Chapter 5:

Ancient Myths from the Ivory Coast

The Ivory Coast, located in West Africa, has been inhabited for thousands of years, and academics believe that they are the ancestors of many present-day ethnic groups such as the Ega, Zehiri, and the Ehotile.

The myths and legends that have survived are wondrous tales meant to captivate and educate, amaze, and strengthen the people's morals and ethics. There are a number of deities, creatures, divine spirits, and even monsters to reinforce the roles of each individual within the community.

The Rebel Girl and the Corpse

Nan Kognon was famous for her incredible beauty. Every man in her community desired her as his wife, but when they asked, she refused to marry any of them, even the strongest and most successful hunter, N'gasselet, on the basis that he had a number of scars upon his body.

One day, a stranger appeared in their lands, one who was just as beautiful as Nan Kognon and whose body wasn't blemished with scars. When she saw him for the first time, she gasped and stated that he was the only man for her and that he would be her husband. She demanded that the tribe start the wedding celebrations, and after the wedding, Nan Kognon left for the marital home with her new husband.

The moment they stepped out of the village, the man took off his boubou (a garment similar to a kaftan), which was particularly fine. When she asked him why, he told her he was hot. They continued walking, and when they arrived at the fork in the road which led to the cemetery, he started to take off his undergarments. When she asked him why, he told her he was hot.

As they entered the cemetery and began walking around its edge, Nan Kognon started to notice a peculiar smell. She turned and saw that her husband's flesh had started decomposing. Scared and shocked, she tried to run away, but he caught her and told her that since she'd chosen and married him, she would stay with him in the cemetery. Her daily task was to pour hot water into his head. Each day her body became thinner, and misery became her constant companion. She started to sing at night.

One night, N'gasselet was attempting to track a buffalo near the river when he heard singing. Leaving the buffalo behind, he started to follow it. When Nan Kognon saw him, she started to beg him to rescue her. N'gasselet agreed and saved her. When she was back in the safety of her family, she vowed she would marry no one but N'gasselet. Taking her as his wife, they had several children.

Honeymoon in the Forest with Python

Once a beautiful young woman lived in a village, her beauty was renowned far beyond her territory. But no matter what her parents or the villagers tried to do, she refused to marry. However, she did swear that if she ever met someone would, she would want to marry, she would put a calabash over her mother's head.

Upon the death of the queen, the village started to arrange the funeral. The queen was so highly regarded that people from far a wide – men, women, children, nobles, and even genies – came to pay their last respects to her. Python desired to go and alter his shape into that of a handsome young man.

One night, the young woman was helping to prepare the evening meal when she looked up and spotted him. Instantly, she placed a calabash over her mother's head, shocking everyone around them.

The young woman married Python. After the funeral, he asked her which road he needed to take.

When he tried to tell her that she needed to stay at home, she refused. Eventually, Python gave up, and they departed from the village.

They journeyed through rivers, through mountains and forests and savannahs, eventually arriving at a very large pit. Python told her that this was his home. Together, they lived there, and the woman bore human children and snake children. Python hunted every day to feed his family and never let them go without.

One day, the young woman's stepmother arrived at their home, although the village and the rest of the family had tried to stop her. Python and the woman welcomed her, and the stepmother helped wash and care for both the snake children and the human children. After six days, the stepmother asked them which road would lead her back home. Python told her the way but warned her not to drink the river water but instead to drink the muddy water.

The stepmother listened and drank the muddy water. When she returned home, her stomach began to hurt, and it wasn't long before she started to vomit. But she vomited gold enough that it filled her home. She gave some to the mother of her stepdaughter.

The woman's mother soon headed straight to her daughter's home, where she was aghast at the thought of her daughter giving birth to snakes. She stayed for four days but refused to help or even touch the snake children. When she asked Python for directions home, he told her the same as he told the stepmother.

However, the mother refused to listen and instead drank her fill of the clean river water. When she arrived at her home, she began to experience its effects and wanted to be sick. She left her home to vomit outside, but Python was lying in wait and killed her. Once she was dead, he took her body to the pit.

There, he asked his wife whether she wanted smooth-skinned or hair-covered prey. She chose the smooth-skinned prey and requested that she took her mother's body back home. But she took a human child and a snake child to accompany her. Along the way, she told her children the situation wasn't anyone's fault but the grandmother's. When Python learned of his wife's unhappiness, he told her to take the human child back home and name him Anini.

Valy, the Difficult Prince and the Lioness

Long ago, the wealthy King Tcheko had a single son named Valy, who he proclaimed the heir to the throne. When the son was old enough, his father tried to convince him to take a wife. He organized a great party and invited every beautiful woman to appear at his palace to help this. Every lovely lady appeared and showed off their charms beneath the king's gaze. But Prince Valy refused them all, finding fault with all of them to the point where the king's nobles declared him to be difficult. However, Prince Valy promised that when he met the right woman, he would marry.

One day, the beautiful woman arrived in the village. She walked around it three times, and every single person spoke loud about her incredible beauty. The prince met with his father and claimed that he would marry her. When his father reminded him that they didn't know anything about her or where she came from. However, the prince refused to listen and wanted to marry her right then and there.

His father sighed and agreed. The marriage took place, and the entire village came to celebrate it. At night, the prince went into the marital home with his new bride. But it didn't take long before he started screaming. Guards rushed into the hut to discover the prince's body, lifeless and torn apart by a lioness who turned around and disappeared into the night.

Chapter 6:

Ancient Myths from Egypt

O ut of all the ancient African civilizations to have emerged through time, Ancient Egypt is perhaps the widest known. There are various reasons for this. Its location within the northern part of the continent allowed it to have access with several other civilizations, such as Mesopotamia, Greece, Rome, etc. They recorded their interactions with Egypt through writings and artwork that have survived, and that its impressive monuments and structures have also withstood time and fighting. Since outside cultures failed to penetrate the Sub-Sahara Desert region, there are not as many ancient writings or depictions of the cultures that flourished there.

The Ancient Egyptian civilization emerged around c. 4,000 BCE, as identified by tomb paintings and burial practices, and continued with the death of Queen Cleopatra VII, who was the last ruler of the Ptolemaic Dynasty. Every single part of Egyptian life – from music to art, from clothing to construction – has been recorded, giving us a fantastic window into this amazing civilization, including their religious beliefs.

There is no other African civilization from the ancient world that has recorded as many myths and legends as the Egyptians. Several creation myths can be seen adorning temples from different time periods, and the dual nature of the gods are clearly identified with the Nile – the River Nile flows through the country, bringing life and prosperity, but like the gods when angered, it could bring floods, devastation, and famine.

The Egyptians went on the influence others through trade. Their myths inspired Greek philosophers such as Plato and Aristotle and were as far-reaching as ancient China when the Silk Road opened in 130 BCE. The concept of reincarnation – a common theme in Egyptian mythology – was influential on Pythagoras in particular, and just like Greece, the ancient Roman religious belief system borrowed heavily from Egypt.

The ancient Egyptians believed that life was just one small part of a journey that continued for eternity and was dictated and influenced by the gods. There were many gods within the Egyptian pantheon; some were depicted as fully human, others with the heads or bodies of animals, and some completely portrayed as animals, reflecting the deep connection they had with the world around them.

Osiris and Set

Together with his sister-wife Isis, Osiris ruled the world with wisdom and justice. Deciding the location on where to plant trees, he directed the course of the River Nile so that the people could live in harmony and have their needs met.

He kept ma'at (harmony) at the heart of all decisions and loved his father and siblings. But his twin brother Set, who was jealous of Osiris even before they were born, did not like all the power and attention he was receiving. In secret, he measured his brother's body and ordered a truly magnificent chest to fit him. Once completed, Set hosted a wondrous banquet. He invited 72 people, including his brother. When the party was finished, he claimed he would gift the beautiful box to the person who fit in it the best. Everyone tried, and when it was his turn, Osiris climbed within, and Set closed it tight. He then tossed the box into the River Nile and proclaimed his brother was dead and that he was now ruler.

However, Isis did not believe that Osiris was dead and began the long, arduous search for her husband. Eventually, she came to Byblos (modern-day Lebanon), where she discovered the chest within a tree. The people of Byblos helped remove the chest from the tree, and for this, Isis gave them her blessing. She then returned to Egypt with her husband's body and started to gather the ingredients for the potion that could revive him. She enlisted her sister Nephthys, the wife of Set, to watch Osiris's body.

Meanwhile, Set was beginning to fear his sister's magical abilities and wondered whether he should try to find the body to prevent Isis from returning him to life. When he discovered that his wife was missing, he searched for her. When he found her, he asked her if she knew where Osiris' body was. She told him that she didn't know, but Set realized that she was lying. He eventually got the information from her and found the location. Once there, he opened the coffin and tore his brother's body into 42 pieces (other sources say 14), and scattered them across the land so that no one could find them. Satisfied, Set went back to the palace.

Isis discovered that the chest had been destroyed and her husband's body had disappeared upon her return. Wracked by guilt, Nephthys informed her sister of what had happened and vowed to aid her in the search to retrieve the pieces of their brother's body. Together, they searched high and low. Each time they discovered a piece of his body, they buried it within the ground and erected a shrine on top so that it would safeguard it from Set. This, in turn, established the 42 provinces of the country.

They found every piece of Osiris' body save for his genitalia, which a fish had consumed. Isis then fashioned a new penis and joined with him, which resulted in a pregnancy. Isis then gave birth to the falcon-headed God, Horus the Younger (not Horus, his brother). Although Isis had revived her husband, Osiris wasn't whole and therefore couldn't be king any longer. Instead, he ventured to the underworld, where he became the just ruler of the dead.

Isis raised Horus in secret, keeping him protected from his uncle Set. When he reached adulthood, Horus arrived at the palace and challenged Set for the kingdom he had stolen away from his brother. Set agreed, and they battled for 80 years until Set was finally defeated. Set was banished to the deserts (some sources claim Set was killed, others claim Horus divided the land for each of them to rule one part), and Horus ruled the country with his mother and aunt as his counselors.

Creation of the Sun

When iu neserer (meaning Island of Flame), the primordial hill emerges from the chaotic waters, the first gods known as the Ogdoad gather to create the sun. They created it by having the Great Cackler, a goose, laying an egg on the hill which came to be identified with Amun.

Esna Cosmogony

Creation myths in ancient Egypt differ depending on the region and the historical period. The Esna creation myth tells that the goddess Neith was the first deity to emerge from Nun's chaotic waters and transformed herself into the shape of a cow to eat the fish in the water. Afterward, she transformed into a human woman and spoke 30 names – these names became 30 deities to help her create the world. Neith then took the essence from within her body and placed it within an egg that hatched the sun god Re (sometimes spelled Ra). Re then named himself Amun and finished creating the world, the gods through his saliva, and mankind through his tears.

Chapter 7:

Mythology from Madagascar

Archaeological evidence shows that the island of Madagascar was inhabited first by foragers around 2000 BCE, although there may be evidence to suggest that humans were visiting as early as the early Holocene, around 10,500 years ago.

However, the earliest settlers seemed to have arrived on the island's shores between 350 BCE and 250 CE and originated from the Sunda Islands in the Malay Archipelago. In the seventh century, Arab traders reached the island, and then around the tenth century, there was a mass migration of Bantu-speaking people from Southeast Africa. Another century later and Madagascar saw another wave of immigrants, this time Tamil-speaking peoples from south India.

All these influences – Asian, African, and Southeast Asian – had a great impact on Madagascans' religious identity, which is reflected in the many myths and legends that have survived.

Lord of the Waters

The Merina are the descendants of the Vizimba, the first settlers, who originated from Borneo. Legends state that Tompondrano is a snake god, the highest of them all, who ruled all the snakes and acted as a messenger between them and the humans, helping to end troubles between them.

A young Vizimba boy was playing with a serpent, a monster who had seven heads. Enjoying the boy's company, the serpent took him to his home beneath the water and refused to let him go. The boy appealed to Tompondrano to rescue him. The snake god told him to be patient and then told Kingfisher to give a message to the boy's parents: they needed to sacrifice a sheep and a chicken to the monster who had their son, and this would convince it to let the boy go.

The parents did as Tompondrano requested, and the seven-headed snake let their son go. To reward Kingfisher for his part, Tompondrano made his wings sparkle and become even more lovely.

Creation

The Betsimisaraka, the second largest ethnic group after the Merina and are descendants of Bantu-speaking Africans and Asian Austronesians, believe that Zanahary is the Supreme Being. A sky deity, he lived by himself and, after realizing that he was lonely, produced Razanajanahary, his son. For a long time, father and son lived together, but Razanajanahary soon became bored and desired to explore what lay beyond their heavenly home.

Zanahary encouraged his son to explore, but he discovered that there wasn't anywhere for him to stand when he attempted to. Informing his father, Zanahary vowed to change this. Taking his knife (a rainbow), he used to cut out pieces of the indefinable mass that swirled beneath the heavens. After a time, when he had numerous pieces, Zanahary then used the rainbow to help him construct the moon and the rest of the heavenly bodies. Then he used piles of the sliced pieces to create the mountains, fashioned valleys and flattened land to make the plains. When this was all done, Razanajanahary got into a basket, and his father lowered him down.

Mahaka and Kotofetsy

Many cultures around Africa feature gods and characters that are known for being either mischievous or tricksters. And, just like elsewhere, their natures can be either revered or criticized.

Mahaka and Kotofetsy were deities known for their quick wits. The Merina people thought so highly of their own intelligence that they would sometimes try to outsmart the gods. One day, Mahaka and Kotofetsy transformed themselves into elderly men and allowed a Merina man to try to trick them. However, they out tricked him and took everything he owned, including the clothes on his back, leaving him to run home naked.

Another myth tells how they tricked a sorcerer into being beaten by his neighbors with large sticks after making them believe he has defiled their family's tomb.

In one myth where Mahaka is alone, the God saw a grouchy old man who did not like to part with his money. Transforming himself into a small child. He continued to harass and annoy the man until he finally snapped and asked what he should do to get a little quiet. Mahaka, still taking the form of a boy, told him that he should make him his heir. The rich man agreed to do so, and upon his death, Mahaka gained all his money.

Chapter 8:

Mythology from Ethiopia

A long with Egypt, Ethiopia has long been a country known to ancient scholars. In particular, the Greeks had a relationship with the Ethiopians. Some of their myths and legends were recorded or infused with Greek stories.

Located in the Horn of Africa, this region of the continent has been inhabited since man's earliest moments. The kingdom of D'mt is the oldest culture to be recorded here, with archaeologists dating it to around the tenth century BCE and flourished until the fifth century BCE. Very few inscriptions have survived, but it is believed that it was an indigenous one, although it was highly probable that the Sabaeans of South Arabia influenced it since they dominated the Red Sea area.

After D'mt fell, various smaller states started to fill the vacuum they left behind. The kingdom of Askum (also known as the Askumite Kingdom or the Kingdom of Axum) emerged in the first century CE in the northern part of the country and flourished until its downfall in the early ninth century. They were great traders, and their cities were vital stops in the Classical World's commercial routes, which allowed them to prosper. Their religious beliefs transformed from a pantheon of gods – including Astar, Mahrem, and Beher - to adopt Christianity in the fourth century (and being the location of the Ark of the Covenant), and then being influenced by Islam in the seventh century, although it didn't last for long.

As a result, numerous myths and legends originate from Ethiopia, but the best known of them all is about Sheba, the beautiful queen.

The Queen of Sheba

In the kingdom of Sheba (located in modern-day Ethiopia), the land was ruled over by a beautiful queen named Makeda. Her kingdom was known for its unique skills and exceptional craftsmanship.

As queen, Mekeda knew her kingdom was strong and wealthy, but when Tamrin, a merchant, informed her about the wise Solomon, king of Israel, and the magnificent temple that he had ordered to be constructed, she decided to pay him a visit.

She gathered up lots of gifts to present to him. She wanted to test him with a series of rather difficult questions until he had satisfied her. When she arrived, she offered him the gifts and stayed up all night talking with him. She decided to stay for a time, and she and Solomon became lovers. Returning home, she discovered that she was pregnant and eventually gave birth to a beautiful baby boy whom she named Menelik.

As Menelik grew older, he started questioning his mother about his father. When he learned it was King Solomon, Menelik ordered a trip and made the journey to Jerusalem. He stayed with his father for a time, and when it was time to return home, he left with additional servants and a priest.

Along the way, this priest informed Menelik that he had stolen the Ark of the Covenant from Solomon's Temple. Once he had found out about this,

Solomon chased after Menelik but couldn't keep up with him.

Menelik decided to keep the Ark in the kingdom and placed it beneath the Saint Mary of Zion Church, where is it is still believed to be today.

Lalibela

In the twelfth century, a beautiful baby boy was born to Jan Seyum, the king of the Zagwe Dynasty, and named Lalibela. A swarm of bees surrounded him but did not sting him, and the people took this as a sign that he would be king one day.

When he was still a young boy, he took a trip to Jerusalem so that he could walk in Jesus' footsteps. During this time, his brother poisoned him with the help of a servant. The poison didn't kill him, however, but his spirit traveled up to Heaven.

While there, God informed him that he needed to construct a New Jerusalem and instructed him to create churches out of the rock in his kingdom. For three days, Lalibela's soul stayed in Heaven before it returned to his body. Upon waking, he informed his family of his new divine mission.

When he returned home, he called for the king-dom's most skilled stonemasons. He told them that they must be the best church they could but refused to let them use bricks, mortar, or wood. The only material they could use was the rock. At first, they thought him insane, that they wouldn't be able to do as he requested.

However, not wanting to disappoint him, as he was now their king, they set about creating the church. They chose a spot within the blazing red hills and began cutting trenches around a piece of solid rock. Slowly, they sculpted and carved the exterior of it, working from top to bottom. When the exterior was complete, they started on the interior. According to legend, as the men slept during the night, angels came down from Heaven to help them.

For twelve years, King Lalibela refused to sleep. Instead, he wanted to stay awake so that he could oversee the project and make sure everything was done to his specified plans. However, he finally gave in and slept; in his dream, he was visited by St. George, who wondered why he hadn't built him a home. Lalibela vowed to construct him a magnif-icent church.

Today, these churches can still be seen.

Creation Myth

In the beginning, Wak was the Supreme Being who created the world and dwelled high in the sky, keeping the heavens safe from Earth by covering them with stars.

When he looked down at the Earth, he saw it was flat and did not like this. So he told Man to create a coffin. When the coffin was finished, he put Man into it and shut the lid on it, sealing Man inside. Placing it into the ground, he sent forth a magnificent firestorm that lasted for seven years, allowing the mountains to form.

Afterward, the fires dissipated, and Wak released Man from the coffin. Man wandered alone until Wak used his blood to make Woman. Together, Man and Woman gave birth to thirty children. Because they had so many, Man became ashamed and hid fifteen of them. Wak, on discovering them, transformed them into demons and animals.

Chapter 9:

Dictionary of African Deities, Demons, Spirits, and Places

A

Aalu – (Egyptian) the paradise land in which Osiris dwelled. To reach here, the souls of the deceased needed to pass through either 15 or 21 gates, which were all guarded by demons.

Aani – (Egyptian) a god with the head of an ape.

Abassi (Efrik) – the creator god and sky God of the Efrik people of Southern Nigeria. Although he didn't want them to, he permitted his two children to go to Earth but insisted on certain rules; they couldn't lay with each other, couldn't engage in agriculture, and returned to heaven to eat. Once on Earth, the children soon became lovers, and their children populated the world. Abassi gifted them with arguing and death and ensured that they would often quarrel and kill each other.

Abatawa – These are fairies who were so small that they could hide within the grass. They shoot poisoned arrows at their enemies and sleep in ant-hills.

Aberewa – (Akan) She was a primordial woman according to the Akan people of Ghana and the Ivory Coast. She pounded maize in her mortar, and her pestle hit the sky. This resulted in the sky god Nyame who moved away. Seeing this, Abere-wa collected several mortar and pestles to reach him. When she ran out, she asked a child to take a mortar and pestle from the bottom which they did, resulting in the entire structure's collapse.

Abommubuwafre – Another name for the sky god Nyame.

Abonsam – an evil spirit who could be scared away by making a great deal of noise.

Abosum – the gods of the Ashanti people of Ghana.

Abuk – (Dinka) – the primordial woman of the Dinka (South Sudan). She lived with her husband, Garang, in a small clay pot eating a single grain of corn each day, but when the lid was removed, they started to grow taller. When she hit the sky with her pestle, the God Deng became annoyed and made grinding harder than before.

Achimi – (Berber) the bull-god of the Kabyle people of Algeria. He was the offspring of Itherther and Thamautz, who drove away from his father and then mated with his sister and mother.

Adama – The husband of Hawa, whom he begot 40 children with. Ashamed, he hid twenty of them from God, but when God discovered them, he took them for himself and used a wall to separate them from their parents.

Adamastor – a terrifying spirit of the Cape of Good Hope.

Adro – the side of the God Adroa as bad. Usually depicted with only half a body and lives within water.

Adroa – the creator god of the Lugbara of Uganda.

B

Ba (Egyptian) – a god manifested in the form of a pharaoh.

Ba (Egyptian) – the soul, and one of the five elements that make up a whole human being. It is depicted as a bird with a human head and flies between this life and the afterlife.

Ba-Maguje – A Hausa (Niger and Nigeria) spirit which causes a person to become so thirsty that they become drunk.

Ba-Pef (Egyptian) – a god of the underworld.

Ba-Toye (Hausa) – a spirit that causes destructive fires.

Baatsi (Efe, Democratic Republic of Congo) – the first man to be created. He wanted to make his wife happy so much that he picked the forbidden tahu fruit. In punishment, God decided that all their descendants should die.

Babi (Egyptian) – a violent god of sexual prowess whose penis acted as the bolt on the door of heaven. Other myths state his penis was used as a mast on the ferry boat of the underworld. He is usually depicted as a baboon with a large, erect penis.

Bagda – a spirit with the ability to control wind and rains.

Baloi – (Zambia) – sorcerers who can perform magic.

Balubaale - - also spelled Balubare, these are nature spirits of the Baganda (Uganda).

Bata (Egyptian) – Bata was a shepherd who lived with his elder brother Anpu and his wife. When his sister-in-law tried to seduce him, he rejected her advances, and she told her husband that he tried to rape her. An ox warned Bata, who then fled, but Anpu chased after him. Crossing the river, the gods made many crocodiles appear in the water so that Anpu couldn't follow after him. Bata then escaped to the land of the acacias, where his soul lived in the flower of one of the trees. The gods presented him with a beautiful wife. When the pharaoh heard of the woman's beauty, he sent her many gifts. She betrayed Bata and went to live in Egypt with the pharaoh. She requested that Bata's tree be cut down, and he died. However, Anpu gathered some seed and immersed it in water, allowing Bata to be reborn as a bull. The pharaoh ordered the slaughter of the bull to please his new consort. When two drops of blood fell beside the city gate's two trees sprung up overnight. Bata was alive in one of the trees. His former wife tried to kill him again by convincing the pharaoh to cut the trees down. When the woodcutter started to fell them, a single chip flew into her mouth, and she swallowed it, instantly becoming pregnant with Bata. When the child grew up, he inherited the pharaoh's throne and made Anpu his heir. He condemned his faithless wife to death.

C

Cannibals – shape-shifting non-humans who eat human flesh. They have elongated thumbnails so they can slice off the flesh, while others are depicted with tails that have an extra mouth on end. Some myths claim they are beautiful young men who seduce women away from their homes and then eat them.

Castle of Light (Kursuri ya Nuru) – An Eastern Paradise where only righteous souls can reach via a ship with a devout captain. One myth says that a blind man named Habbat-ar-Rumani found seven doves, one of which was also blind. One of the doves discovered a magic herb that gave both man and bird back their sight, and they all lived within the Castle of Light.

Cedar of the End (Swahili-speaking kingdoms) – A divine tree. Each leaf, which is large enough for an angel to kneel upon it, has an individual's name written on it. When a leaf breaks off and falls onto the ground, an angel will seek out that individual and inform them that their time on Earth is finished.

Chichinguane (Mozambique) – A young girl who the fish Chipfalmfula swallowed to save her after she waded within a river. She stayed within his belly until she became an adult and was ready to marry. When she stepped onto dry land, a pack of ogres attacked her. Chipfalmfula stopped the course of the river with his gigantic body so that she could cross safely and then drowned the ogres.

Later, she met and married a handsome prince who fell in love with her.

D

Dama Ngile – Meaning 'Great Bull,' he was the son of Daibu and demanded that King Sunjata give him the magic sword (also named Dama Ngile). The sword rose from the pile of weapons without anyone touching it. Later, he became king of Jerre.

Dan Ayido Hwedo (Yoruba/Nigeria) – Meaning 'Rainbow Snake,' he was a divine serpent created by Mawu who would transport the sky god when he visited Earth. Mawu used the snake's excreta to form the mountains. After the world was completed, Dan Ayido Hwedo coiled his body up beneath the sea in order to support the earth. Whenever he moves, earthquakes cause the land to shudder. When he has finished eating all the iron within the seas, he will start to eat himself, starting at his tail, until there is nothing left, and the earth will collapse into the sea.

Dibobia (Congo and Gabon) – An ancient spider that hung between heaven and Earth and helped God Mebega to create the world.

Dodo (Southern Africa) – A Bushman witch or demon.

Dogir (Egypt) The Dogir were Nubian spirits who lived in the River Nile and were said to have been human originally until witches transformed them. Some would marry and impregnate humans. Some myths claim they were hideous beings who lived normal human lives during the day but transformed into wolves at night.

Dongo (Nigeria) – an ancient storm god of the Songhai people. When he threw an ax, a huge bolt of lightning tore through the land and killed several men. Taking some water, he sprayed their bodies with it and brought them back to life.

E

Eda Male (Yoruba/Nigeria) – idols of twins and are commonly used in initiation ceremonies.

Edeke – a destructive god of the Teso people of Uganda.

Edjo (Egypt) – Known as the Lady of Heaven, Queen of Gods, and Uadjit, she was a cobra goddess of the Lower Kingdom. She originated as the goddess of the primordial darkness and then became the Horus and Bast's nurse. Pharaohs used to adorn their crowns with the uraeus to honour the goddess.

Efe (Pygmies/Congo basin) – the first man and the son of Matu. When he was born, a monster swallowed his parents, but Efe destroyed it and released them. He was carried to Heaven, where he stayed with the gods and became a hunter. Later, he returned to Earth with three magic spears.

Ehlose – a guardian spirit who warns their charge whenever there is danger.

Eight Ancestors (Dogon) – the four sets of twins born to the first man and woman created by Anma.

Ekera – the Ethiopian underworld.

Ekko (Ethiopia) – a spirit of a deceased person known to possess humans.

Elephantine Triad (Egypt) – a group of deities consisting of the God Khnum and the two goddesses Sati and Anuket.

Emadloti (Swazi) – Ancestors of the Swazi who have influence over their descendants.

Emeli Hin (Berber) – a creator god of the Berber group, Tuareg.

Emi (Yoruba, Nigeria) – one of the three spirits that live within each human being and is the force of each breath.

Erosi (Egbo, Nigeria) – spirits of fertility and prosperity.

Eshu (Yoruba, Nigeria) – A god of fate, a messenger god, and an angel-trickster. He was an attendant of the God Fa and was responsible for opening his eyes each day. He hated having to serve Orisha so much that he rolled a large boulder onto his house, which killed him and split his body into 401 pieces. One myth claims that he was able to persuade the sun and moon to swap jobs for a single day, which caused chaos throughout the land.

F

Fan (Benin) – the Fon god of destiny who was said to have 16 eyes and dwelled within a palm tree in the sky. Every day, the God Eshu opened his eyes. He was the son of Minona.

Fara Maka (Mali) – a legendary hero who attacked the hippopotamus Mali, who had consumed the land's crops, with a spear. Unfortunately, Mali ate him as well. His wife used magic to paralyze the monster.

Faran Maka (West Africa) – a hero of the Songhai people. When Zin-Kibaru, a water spirit, caused the fish to eat all his people's rice, Faran Maka attacked the spirit and took his magical musical instrument. He possessed a huge beard which he used to catch fish and ate a hippopotamus each day. He found a young woman in a termite hill and by her had two children, Weikare and Wango.

Faro (West Africa) – A water god of the Bambara people and the twin brother of Pemba. He and his brother were born from the seeds which were sown at the four corners of the world. He created calm and order out of chaos, created the heavens, killed the spirit of the hot winds Teliko, and then impregnated himself to produce the first humans. He bore twins and gave them the power of speech.

Fatouma – A princess who Hammadi saved just before the Dragon of the Lake was about to eat her. She went on to marry him.

Fidi Mukullu (Zaire) – a creator god.

G

Ga-gorib (Western Cape) – Also known as Gama or Goub, he was a monster who used to throw people into large pits. Eventually, Heitsi-eibib killed him in the same way. Another legend says it was the trickster god, Jackal, who killed him.

Garamas (Sahara region) – the first man according to the Garamantes.

Gassire - The son of Nganamba, he learned the song of the birds. When his lyre was dipped into the blood of his sons, fallen during battle, he sang the epic song, the Dausi.

Gate of Way (Egypt) – the entrance to the Western Desert.

Gauna (Southern Africa) – the ruler of the spirits of the dead within the Bushman mythology.

Gaunab (Western Cape) the Hottentot god of the darkness. He fought Tsunigoab for supremacy but lost and was exiled.

Gbade (the kingdom of Dahomey) – a thunder god who used lightning as his weapon to kill those who do wrong. Any man who is killed in this matter will have his possessions scattered across the road, and if anyone touches them, they will be killed the same way.

Gbeni (Sierra Leone) – the supreme spirit of the Mende people.

Gborogboro (Uganda) – an ancestor of the Lugbara.

Gewi (Southern Africa) – the son of Kaang and Coti who went to Earth to teach the Bushmen how to dry roots.

Gibini (Uganda) – a god of plague.

Gihanga (Rwanda) – an ancient king and the son of Kigwa and invented metal-working art.

Gindr (Uganda) – the supreme God of the Lendu people.

Gizo (Nigeria), also known as Yoruba Anansai, was a trickster-hero depicted as a spider and Koki consort.

H

Ha (Egypt) – Known as the Lord of the Libyans, he was the guardian of the desert.

Ha (Egypt) – One of the five elements that make up a complete being.

Hah (Egypt) – the male personification of eternity and infinity, who is typically depicted as holding up the heavens with his raised arms and clutching a palm-frond.

Hai-uri (West Africa) – a monster with only half a body. He would gather victims and then take them down to the underworld.

Hale (Sierra Leone) – the magic used by the Mende people.

Ham – the son of Noah whose skin was transformed to black in punishment for not doing as his father ordered and having sex with his wife while they were in the Ark. He then became king of Egypt, and his sons went on to populate the African continent.

Hamti (Egypt) – a farmer who stole a donkey and the possessions it was carrying from its peasant owner. The peasant asked the landowner Meritensa, who was also a judge, for help, and so he brought the matter to the king. The king was so impressed by the elegance of the peasant's speech that he ordered Meritensa to confiscate the farmer's property and to compensate the peasant.

Hap (Egypt) - also spelled Hap or Haapi, he was a fertility god and a god of the Nile. Depicted as an androgynous figure, he was responsible for the Nile flooding. He was born when lightning or moonbeams impregnated a virgin cow. He also aided Isis and Nepythys in bringing Orisi back to life by suckling him. He was the consort of Mut and Nekhbet and was sometimes depicted as a goose with two heads.

I

I Kaggen (Southern Africa) – another name for the Busham god, Kaang, in the form of a spirit of the praying mantis.

Iampelamananoro (Madagascar) – a beautiful maiden who was held captive by Raivato. The hero Iboniamasiboniamanoro rescued her and hammered Raivato into the ground.

Iboniamasiboniamanoro (Madagascar) – a hero. His mother sought advice on how to conceive from Ranakombe, a seer. She journeyed up to Heaven, where a grasshopper entered her body and dwelled within her uterus for ten years. Inside her, her unborn child got his mother to swallow a knife. He then used it to cut himself out of her womb, who subsequently died. Iboniamasibonia-manoro jumped into a fire, but the flames did not hurt him. He died a few years after rescuing Iampelamananoro.

Idlozi (South Africa) the guardian spirit that watches over a Zulu individual.

Ihy (Egypt) – also spelled Ify, Ahy, and Herusmatauy, Ihy was a god of music and Horus and Hathor's son.

Ijuru (Rwanda) – a realm in the sky.

Ikenga (Nigeria) – a god of fortune.

Ilaansai (Tanzania) – the supreme God of the Fipa people.

Ilat (Kenya, Uganda) – a rain god and the son of Tororut and Seta. He is responsible for carrying water to his father, but each time he spills some, it falls as rain.

Ilomba (Zambia) – a being with a serpent's body and the head of a human who sucks the blood of its master's enemies. When it is killed, the master will die.

Imilozi (South Africa) – ancestor sprits of the Zulu. Translating as 'whistlers,' their job was to exchange the secrets of the gods to humans, but they couldn't understand their whistling language and so couldn't tell them what they knew.

J

Jah't (Egypt) - a moon god also known by Joh, who later merged with Thoth.

Jakuta (Nigeria) – a god of thunder.

Jaliya (Nigeria) – a beautiful young woman whose friends shoved her into a river where she discovered a palace. There, she found its king – a serpent. When she started singing to the serpent, a real king named Gongola heard her and drained the river to find her. The serpent slithered away, and she married the king.

Jata – also known as Janziri and Nakada, Jata is a spirit that causes insanity and venereal diseases.

Jinde Sirinde – she was dragged to the river and forced to marry Waterlord. When she called her lover to help rescue her, he killed Waterlord by decapitating his seven heads.

Jnun (Morocco) – a demon often depicted in the form of a toad.

Jok (Uganda) – a creator and rain god of the Alur people.

Jokinam (East Africa) – a lake god who is said to own a large herd of cows grazing on the bed of Lake Albert. He is tended to by the fishermen who have drowned within its waters.

Jokrut (Uganda) – the God of twins of the Alur people.

Jolima – a hero who escorted a group of women home at night against a pack of hyenas. His strength and bravery were so strong that the hyena couldn't hurt him. Instead, Jolima caught him and paraded him around the village as a trophy.

Juko (Uganda) – a hero king of the Buganda people. When he enraged a priest, the sun hid from the world, plunging the land into darkness. Eventually, a lake god helped bring the sun back to its rightful place.

K

Ka (Egypt) – one of the five elements that make up an entire, whole person. It was believed that an individual's ka would live on after the person had died, and so the people offered it food and drink to sustain it.

Ka Tyeleo (Ivory Coast) – a creator god.

Kaang (Southern Africa) – the supreme God of the Bushmen, the husband of Coti, and the father of Cogaz and Gewi. An ogre swallowed him but was vomited up without any harm. After some thorns pricked him and resulted in his death, ants ate his flesh. Still, he was able to resurrect himself. He took an old shoe and created the moon from it, and had the ability to transform shoes into dogs that could attack his enemies. All his magical abilities reside in a single tooth.

Kaba (Tanzania, Uganda, Kenya) – the first village established by the humans who left the sky with Faro.

Kabundungulu – the son of Nzuadia and the twin brother of Sudika-mbambi. When he and his brother emerged from their mother's womb, they were already fully formed. Kimbuji, a fish, swallowed his brother whole, and so Kabundungulu rescued him. However, he soon grew jealous of the fact that Sudika-mbambi had two wives when he didn't have one. The two brothers fought and decided to go their separate ways. Another myth states that they married the two sisters of the king of the underworld.

Kaikara (Uganda) – a goddess of the harvest worshipped by the Banyoro people.

Kaiwan (Ethiopia) – an earth goddess, a goddess of plenty.

L

Labama – the daughter of Nchienge and the sister-wife of Woto.

Lagarre – an African prince who became king on his father's deathbed since his older brothers were lazy and incompetent. Lagarre ordered a vulture to travel to heaven in order to bring back Tabele, the royal drum. When Lagarre hit the drum, a new city rose out of the desert, which was guarded by a fearsome dragon named Bida. Lagarre was permitted to enter the city and become its king only on the promise that he would offer a young girl to the dragon each year. Upon the sacrifice, the dragon would fly over the city, named Wagadoo, and vomit gold all over the streets.

Legba (Nigeria) – a god of destiny and an angel-trickster of the Fon people. He was the son of Lisa and Mawu or Minona.

Lepidotus (Egypt) – a sacred fish.

Leza (Zambia) – a creator and sky god of the Kaonde people in Zambia. He gifted men three gourds to take care of the honeybird, including one that shouldn't have been opened until he came down to Earth. However, the honeybird opened the one that he shouldn't, and he released all the ills that afflict the world, while the other two contained seeds.

Lianja (Democratic Republic of the Congo) – a god of the Nkundo people, the son of Itonde and Mbombe, the twin brother and consort of Ntsongo, and the father of Likinda. His father was the first man and reborn as Lianja. He emerged from his mother's thigh, fully formed with his twin sister and immediately climbed onto the roof of the house so he could watch over his kingdom. He sent the sun-bird Nkundo to retrieve the sun back from heaven.

M

Ma'at (Egypt) – meaning 'truth,' she was a goddess of justice and truth, the ruler of the underworld, the daughter of Re (Ra), and the wife of Thoth. She was typically depicted as wearing one ostrich feather in which she uses to weigh the souls of the dead.

Ma Kiela (Central Africa) – a mortal woman who became a goddess. She is the queen of women who were killed by a knife.

Maa (Egypt) – the female personification of sight.

Maat (Egypt) – the goddess Atet in the shape of a cat.

Macardit (Sudan) – a Dinka god of misfortune.

Madlebe (Swaziland) - a hero-king and the brother of Madlisa. When he was born, he wore a bracelet that cried tears of blood every time the boy wept. Upon breaking a pot that his father had forbidden him to touch, Madlebe was sent to be executed, but a terrible thunderstorm frightened the executioner, and so the boy was able to escape. When his father died, he returned home and became king.

Mafdet (Egypt) - also known as the Lady of the Castle of Life, was a goddess who protected humans from scorpions and snakes. She is usually depicted as a lynx or panther.

Maghegh (Mali, Niger, Libya) – A Tuareg jinn who impregnated seven virgins who gave birth to seven sons. When they were old enough, he taught them all the necessary skills they would need to become the founders of the seven tribes.

Manhungu (Uganda) – the first being. This being was described as a two-headed androgynous person who later separated to form the male Lumbu and the female Muzita.

N

Na Ngutu (Uganda) – a Bakongo god of the dead.

Nabende (Uganda) – the supreme deity.

Naete (Benin) – a sea deity, the twin sister of Agbe and the mother of Afrikete.

Nagadya (Uganda) – a goddess of the Baganda. She was the wife of B'ima, and the mother of Anantaraja by Ananataboga.

Bagawonyi (Uganda) - a goddess of hunger.

Nai (Ghana) – an ocean god of the Gan people and the father of Ashiakle.

Nakwube (Kenya) – the supreme God.

Nambalista (Namibia, Angola) – the first man according to the Ambo. He ermeged from an egg and soon grew up to be a mighty warrior. When he proclaimed that he had produced himself, his real creator, the God Kalunga, became angry. They met on the battlefield, and Kalunga imprisoned him within a sealed room. However. Nambalista asked the animals for help, and they aided in his escape.

Nana (Nigeria) – an earth goddess of the Yoruba. She was the wife of Obaluwaye and the mother of Omulu.

Nana Buluku (Uganda) – the androgynous deity of the Fon people and who produced the creator god, Mawu-Lisa.

Nandi Bear – also known as Chemosit, Nandi Bear was a man-eating monster in the form of a bear. He is described as half-man, half-bird, with one leg and a mouth that glows in the dark in some accounts.

Nau (Egypt) – a deity with the head of a frog.

Naunet (Egypt) – a goddess of the primordial waters. Together with Nun, she represents the depths of these waters. She is typically portrayed as having the head of a snake, others as a baboon.

O

Obe (Lesotho, South Africa) – familiars of Besuto witches who take the form of large animals.

Obang (Cameroon) – an ancient supreme god.

Obassi (Nigeria) – an ancient supreme god.

Obatala (Nifgeria) – an ancient fertility god and sculptor God of the Yoruba. He was the brother and husband of Oduduwa and the husband of Yemoja, according to other sources.

Obeah – an ancient animal said to kidnap women for witches.

Obosum (Nigeria) – an ancient Ashanti god; also a name for a group of minor deities.

Ochiliombra – in ancient Angolan mythology, this was the soul that was often seen as an individual's shadow. When a person died, the soul leaves the body and becomes a ghost known as an ocilulu.

Oduduwa (Nigerian) - an ancient creator goddess and war goddess. She was the daughter of either Olodumare or Obatala and the mother of Yemoja, Ogun, and Aganju. The Yoruba see her as the founder of their people. In some myths, she was male and the son of Lamurudu, who married Aje and fathering Oranyan. Other stories claim she is female, and her role is to plant the seeds her father gave her on Earth. She then became the wife of Orishako.

Ody andoha – a magical charm designed to prevent the wearer from having headaches.

Ogo (East Africa) – also known as Yurugu, Ogo was an evil god of the Dogon and the son of Amma and the brother of Yasigi. He and his brother were born from one of the two yolks of the primeval egg. From the other yolk came forth the twins Nunmo.

P

Pa-hra (Egypt) – one of the most ancient deities and the father of Ahi.

Pachet (Egypt) – an early goddess of the desert often depicted as a lion.

Pakhet (Egypt) – a god of the hunt.

Pale Fox (East Africa) – an ancient hero of the Dogon people. When he stole seeds from the God Amma, he was exiled, but he left his tracks in the dirt in the form of pawprints, which the people used in divination.

Patakoi (Egypt) – deformed but benevolent beings who were the children of the God Ptah. Phoenician sailors, in particular, would carry carved images of them as good luck charms.

Patek (Egypt) – a protective spirit.

Pemba (Mali) – an ancient creator god and the tree god of the Bambara people. Pemba was born of the void and fashioned the world. He started life on Earth as a seed that grew into an acacia tree. He fashioned Musso-koroni, the first woman, with the wood from his tree. Together, they produced the first humans and animals. She then planted him in the ground and his brother, Faro the water god, dug him up.

Petbe (Egypt) – a god of revenge.

Petsuchos (Egypt) – a crocodile god.

Psille – an ancient race of African people who were able to cure snakebites with a simple touch.

Ptah (Egypt) – a creator god and the patron god of Memphis, artists and craftsmen, and the God of property. He was one of the three Lords of Destiny, and the husband of Sakhmet, and the father of Nefertum. He was born from an egg laid by the Nile Goose (other sources claim he was born from the mouth of Amun, or that he was the son of Nun and Naunet). He created the world by shaping clay, created the gods by thinking of them, then speaking their names aloud, and made mankind from precious metals.

Q

Qahu (Egypt) – a city where the gods reside.

Qamatha (South Africa) – a creator god of the Xhosa people. He sent Chameleon to tell the Xhosa that he will make them immortal. However, Lizard discovered this message and rushed to the people and told them the opposite. When Chameleon arrived, they did not believe him, and, as a result, they stayed mortal.

Qamate – an ancient supreme god.

Qandisa (Morocco) – a water demon who seduces men and drives them insane.

Qebsehsenuf (Egypt) – the falcon (sometimes hawk) headed God who was the son of Horus and was one of the four Amenti. He was the guardian of the west and the intestines (although other sources claim he was the guardian of the liver and gall bladder).

Qedeshet (Egypt) – Known as the Lady of the Heaven, Mistress of the Gods, she was the goddess of health and Min's consort. Eventually, she became an aspect of the goddess Hathor. She was generally depicted as a naked woman holding a lotus flower, a mirror, and snakes while standing on a lion.

Qeh (Egypt) – one of a pair of deities (the other being Qerhit) who were created from Chaos.

Quamta (South Africa) – the ancient and supreme God of the Xhosa.

R

Ra (Egypt) – a creator god, a sun god, and a god of the underworld. He was the father and husband of Hathor, and the father of Isis, Osiris, Nepythys, and Set by Nut, and the father of Ihy by Hathor. Some myths say he emerged by himself from Nun's waters, others that he emerged from the first lotus flower, and others that he was the son of Nut and that he was the father of Shu and Tefnut. Another version claims that he came out of an egg laid by the God Geb while in the form of a goose. He created the first humans using his own tears when Shu and Tefnut finally reappeared. However, he started to believe that mankind was plotting his death, so he sent the goddess Hathor in the form of a lion to slaughter them. She started to enjoy the death and destruction that she was causing, so Ra flooded the land with khakadi, red beer, which she thought was blood. Drinking it, she became intoxicated, and while she was sleeping, Ra took her back. When Isis wanted to discover his real name, she gathered a drop of his saliva and fashioned a snake from it. It bit Ra and caused him pain. Isis cured him of this, and in gratitude he told her his true name – Ran.

Rainbow Monster (Kenya) – a water monster who emerged at night to eat both humans and men. It' is reflected in the sky by a rainbow.

Raluvimbha (South Africa) – an ancient creator god of the Baventa people.

Rang (Sudan) – also known as Garung, he was a god of the hunt.

Ratovoantany (Madagascar) – an ancient creator god who fashioned the first humans from clay before Zanahary breathed life into them. According to myths, he emerged out of the ground like a plant.

S

Sa (Sierra Leone) – an ancient creator god of the Kono people. Myths tell that he lived within the primordial swamp. He was one of two creator gods, the other being Alatangana, who formed land and vegetation. He then eloped with sa's daughter and gave birth to the first humans – four pairs of white children and three pairs of black children, each pair speaking a different language.

Saa (Egypt) – a child of the sun god Ra.

Sabra (Egypt) – a pharaoh's mortal daughter, was rescued by a dragon by a saint and then married him.

Sag (Ethipioa) – a demon that causes drought. He was depicted as having the body of a lioness, a tail with a lotus flower on the end, and a hawk's head.

Sah (Egypt) – the male personification of the constellation Orion. He was the husband of Sopdet and the father of Soped.

T

Ta-Bitjet (Egypt) – a scorpion goddess who was a consort of Horus.

Tachi – a mischievous god who could only be seen to marry a woman with whom he consorted with. Any children born of his union with them are said to be deformed.

Taiki (Nigeria) – A Hausa spirit who caused stomach ailments.

Tamukujen (Ethiopia) – the supreme God of the Didinga people.

Tano (Ghana, Ivory Coast) – a river god of the Akan people and an ancient sun god who was also the brother of Bia. He should have been given the deserts to rule, but instead, he disguised himself as his brother and received the fertile parts of the Earth to rule over.

Tar (Nigeria) – an ancient earth god.

Tari – (Southern Africa) – a spirit who can possess humans.

Tasenetnofret (Egypt) – a goddess and consort of Haroeris, who later merged with Hathor.

Tauetona (Botswana) – the first man who lived in a cave known as Lowe in the heart of the country.

Tauret (Egypt) – also known as Apet, Beset, Epet, Heret, Opet, Rer, Tie, and many others, Tauret was the goddess of childbirth and depicted as having the head of a hippopotamus, the legs of a lion, and the tail of a crocodile. Her appearance was so terrifying that it scared off evil spirits when a child was born. She was originally married to Bes, but later myths state that Set won her from Bes, and she was in charge of souls preparing to be reborn.

U

Uasar (Egypt) – another name for Osiris for the period when he was sleeping during the winter months.

Uchak (Uganda, Democratic Republic of the Congo) – a legendary king who, when he died, was found to have stones in his heart. They were then boiled in oil and used in a ceremony to make it rain.

Udjat (Egypt) – Known more commonly as the Eye of Ra, the Eye of Horus, or the Eye of Atum, this was a third eye that sat in the center of the God's head and symbolized eternity.

Udot (Egypt) – a cobra goddess.

Ugatya – an incubus that was depicted as a snake.

Uh Panga Lwe Zizwe (Southern Africa) – the reed from which the Zulu people emerged from.

Uhlathu Yesizibi (Southern Africa) – the son of a legendary king and queen. A gigantic snake emerged from the queen as she gave birth; when the skin peeled away, it revealed five girls and five boys, with Uhlathu Yesizibi as the first boy.

Uneg (Egypt) – this plant-god holds up the heavens.

V

Velo men (Madagascar) – a legendary race of men created by the supreme God after breathing life into small figures made of clay.

Vere – in Pokono lore, Vere (also spelled Were) was the first man.

Vigara – the first husband of Nyavirungu.

Vorunmila (Nigeria) – an ancient god of the Yoruba.

W

Wadjet (Egypt) – also known as the Lady of Heaven, was a snake goddess and Lower Egypt's patron goddess. She is usually depicted as a fire-breathing cobra that symbolises the sovereignty of the pharaoh. She created the papyrus swamps and suckled the young God Horus. She was the sister of Nekhbet and the mother of Nefertum.

Wai (Zaire) – an ancient sun god and the father of Mokele.

Waka (Ethiopia) – an ancient creator god who founded the Galla tribe. He created the first man and then used a drop of his blood to create woman. They had thirty children, but when Waka asked to see them, the man hid fifteen of them. The children who they hid became the ancestors of all the demons and animals in the world while the others became the ancestors of humans.

X

Xewioso – an ancient thunder god as well as a fertility god.

Y

Yaaru (Egypt) – the fields of the afterlife. They are a peaceful place where sheaths of wheat grow taller than a man. They were situated in the lowest part of the realm of the dead, named Amenti.

Yah (Egypt) – an ancient moon goddess.

Yakombra – a god of morals also known as Nzakombra.

Yansan (Nigerian) – an ancient Yoruba god of the wind.

Yaro (Ethiopia) – a creator god also known as Yero.

Yasigi (East Africa) – according to Dogon mythology, Yasigi was born from one of two yolks of the primordial egg laid by the God Amma. She laid with her twin brother Ogo and populated the world.

Z

Zamba – the supreme God of the Yuande people and the father of Ngi, Nkokn, Otkut.

Conclusion

African mythology is a testament to the rich and varied history of a continent that gave birth to every person on this planet. From the dawn of mankind's history, this vast region has seen human life in its infancy to witness its glorious achievements.

Civilizations have risen to staggering heights only to fall and disappear. The religious beliefs of thousands, perhaps even more than a million ethnic groups and kingdoms, have shaped the course of human history. Most people around the world may recognize ancient Egypt, but Carthage's glorious kingdoms were just as influential on the Classical World as Egypt had been thousands of years earlier.

D'mt was the first kingdom to emerge in Ethiopia, constructing a magnificent temple at modern-day Yeha around 700 BCE. We know that the Sabaeans had an influence over them, although it is still uncertain as to how much. But the kingdom of D'mt was a major power in its own right and continued to flourish until its eventual demise. Not much is known about it, with few excavations revealing this unique culture's social and religious beliefs.

Other kingdoms rose and fell – Askum, Punt, Nubia, Ghana, Mali, and many more – and while their legacies and myths may not be as well recorded as the Egyptians, countless deities, spirits, and legendary figures continue to survive to this day.

Unlike that of Ra, Bast, Hathor, and the rest of the Egyptian deities, deities such as Yansan, Tar, Oduduwa, and many more, are still worshipped. Instead of being recorded on the walls of grand temples or written within books or scrolls, these ancient beings who saw the birth of some most amazing and often overlooked civilizations are worshipped today by modern Africans.

The myths of ancient Africa continue to be told.

References

Barrow, Jim. *African Mythology.*

Bernard, Bernard. *African Mythology: A Concise Guide to the Gods, Heroes, Sagas, Rituals and Beliefs of the African Myths.*

Punch, Geraldine. *Egyptian Mythology.*

Printed in Great Britain
by Amazon